YOUR KNOWLEDGE HAS VALUE

Stanko Radmilovic

Financial Revolution, rapid financial development. Would scientific authority mitigate premature praise?

GRIN Verlag

Bibliografische Information der Deutschen Nationalbibliothek:

Die Deutsche Bibliothek verzeichnet diese Publikation in der Deutschen National-
bibliografie; detaillierte bibliografische Daten sind im Internet über http://dnb.d-
nb.de/ abrufbar.

Imprint:

Copyright © 2013 GRIN Verlag GmbH
Druck und Bindung: Books on Demand GmbH, Norderstedt Germany
ISBN: 978-3-656-59154-2

This book at GRIN:

http://www.grin.com/en/e-book/267625/financial-revolution-rapid-financial-deve-
lopment-would-scientific-authority

GRIN - Your knowledge has value

Der GRIN Verlag publiziert seit 1998 wissenschaftliche Arbeiten von Studenten, Hochschullehrern und anderen Akademikern als eBook und gedrucktes Buch. Die Verlagswebsite www.grin.com ist die ideale Plattform zur Veröffentlichung von Hausarbeiten, Abschlussarbeiten, wissenschaftlichen Aufsätzen, Dissertationen und Fachbüchern.

Visit us on the internet:

http://www.grin.com/

http://www.facebook.com/grincom

http://www.twitter.com/grin_com

Prof. dr Stanko Radmilovic, Novi Sad, Serbia

"Financial Revolution", "rapid financial development" - would now scientific authority mitigate premature praise?

The article was published in the Serbian language, on the site http://radmilovicstanko.com/ with title
"Finansijska revolucija", "rapidni finansijski razvoj"... – da li bi danas naučni autoriteti ublažili preuranjene hvalospeve?

There is almost no dispute about that in the past few decades there has been great, "dramatic", "fundamental", "revolutionary" changes in the world of finance, which many authors call the "new" financial "revolution". These changes have led to the modern financial world changed drastically, that is unrecognizably different from the one of the only 30 days - 50 years.

Increasingly, we meet the term "financial world". It is used as a synonym for Finance to refer to the fact that they gained greater individuality than they had before, when they been encompassed, too, eith the colloquial notion of "world money". However, the notion "World Money" and "World Finance", althoughi closely, not identical. But neither quite different: the world of money and financial world can be said to have been part of the same, but also that each of them is different (narrower and / or wider) than the other. Compiled term "World Money and Finance" is comprehensive, but it is enough pleonastic and thus not absolutely accurate.

***

Nobel laureate Robert C. Merton (1995) speaks of the great, "revolutionary changes" that led to all - to the users of financial services, the producers of financial services and products to persons performing surveillance and control in the financial system.

> MERTON, R. C. (1995): "Financial Innovation and the Management and Regulation of Financial Institutions", Journal of Banking and Finance 19, 461-481; and National Bureau of Economic Research Working Paper 5096 (April 1995)

***

Even before mentioned Mertono's work, at the beginning of the nineties, many other authors have amounted to the same or similar notions. Among them Frederic Mishkin (1990), who is from the September 2006, the member of the Board of Governors of the Federal Reserve USA. He points out that the earlier (before the 1990. when he wrote it), the financial markets and institutions[j] in the U.S. have undergone revolutionary changes, which resulted in the fact that many financial instruments and institutions, who at that time were taken as a given, twenty, or even ten years ago, did not exist.

> *Financial markets and institutions in the United States have been undergoing revolutionary changes in recent years. Twenty, or even ten years ago, many of the financial instruments and institutions that we now take for granted did not exist.*

> *Starting in the 1960s, individuals and financial institutions operating in financial markets in the United States were confronted with drastic changes in the economic environment: Inflation and*

interest rates climbed sharply and became harder to predict, while computer technology advanced rapidly.

Mishkin Frederic, S. (1990), "Financial Innovation and Current Trend in U.S. Financial Markets", National Bureau of Economic *Research*, Working Paper No. 3323, April 1990

***

Martin Hellwig, also points to the fact that in the past few decades has been a financial revolution, and notes that it started in the USA. According to him, the financial revolution has occurred in the period since the mid-seventies to mid-eighties, was launched with local innovations that have arisen in response to the unadjusted regulation of interest rates in times of high inflation.

Hellwig, M. (2003), Comments of Rajan, R. G., Zingales, L. (2003), "Banks and Markets: The Changing Character of European Finance", in: V. Gaspar, P. Hartmann, O. Sleijpen (eds.), The Transformation of the European Financial System, European Central Bank, Frankfurt.

***

How is the financial world changed and can sense a lot of euphoric statements by Robert L. McDonald (2003) on the characteristics of the changes in the world of finance and capital markets. Although McDonald's has primarily focused on U.S. financial syistem and only at the microeconomic level, without any reservations he streses assessment that the (whole) world of finance and capital undergone startling changes in the past thirty years. Ordinary shares and bonds now look almost like something outdated compared to the brilliant, impressive, mysterious world of futures, options, swaps and other new financial products.... Financial markets have actually enormous, often incalculable impact on everyday life.

Robert L. McDonalds, (2003) "Derivative Markets", ch. 1 - Introduction to derivatives, *Pearson plc company*, London

***

In order to perceive the depth and width of the transformation of the world of finance, beside micro financial practice and theory, of great importance are the changes on the macro-national level, but and in countries within some regional and other groupings. In this respect, one should bear in mind, for example, estimations of the financial analysts Edey and Hviding, within the OECD (1995), about it that the financial systems of the countries included in that organization, during past two decades, undergone "comprehensive structural changes".

Financial systems in OECD countries during the past two decades have undergone extensive structural change as a result of regulatory reform and technological innovation. The systems prevailing in most countries in the early 1970s were characterised by important restrictions on market forces which included controls on the prices or quantities of business conducted by financial institutions, restrictions on market access, and, in some cases, controls on the allocation of finance among competing borrowers. These regulatory systems had evolved to serve a number of social and economic policy objectives of governments. Direct controls were used in many countries to allocate finance to preferred industries during the post-war reconstruction period; specialised credit institutions have also been in place to ensure access to credit by smaller enterprises; restrictions on market access and competition were partly motivated by a concern for financial stability; protection of small savers with limited financial knowledge was an important objective of controls on banks; and controls on banks and financial institutions were frequently used as instruments of macroeconomic management.

Edey, M. and K. Hviding (1995), "An Assessment of Financial Reform in OECD Countries", *OECD Economics Department Working Papers*, No. 54

***

Major "structural changes" are really running in the USA eliminating some forms of state regulation in the field of securities 1975. and the main wave of such financial reforms in many other countries there are mid osamadesetih. A typical example is the familiar "big-bang"[i] (big shock) in England. In continental Europe, the reform followed a little later (in the late eighties and the nineties), and in particular the major financial changes in European OECD countries occurred at the constitution of the European Monetary Union (Maastricht agreement signed in 1992. years) and the introduction of the Euro currency, 1. January 1999. which entered into force, and denoted the cessation validity of the previous regimes of national currencies 1. July 2002.

However, far from being a revolutionary change occurred only at the microeconomic level and macro finances of National financial systems, than and in regional and global frameworks such as the European Union; but the world of finance is not equally dramatically transformed in international and global dimensions, although the global financial internationalization, among others, emphasized by the World Bank.

Over the last two decades, the financial markets of leading industrial countries have melded into a global financial system, permitting ever-larger amounts of capital to be allocated not only to their economies, but also to developing and transition economies.

World Development Report za 1990-2000 godinu (chapter 3).

As can be seen, this Bretton Woods financial institution, notes that over the last two decades the financial markets leading industrial countries merged into the global financial system[iii] allowing increasing amounts capital to be allocate not only for their economies than also emerging economies and transition economies.

WE WILL NOT HERE REPEAT OF WHAT WE HAVE SAID IN MANY OTHER PLACES ON MY SITES, BUT THIS IS A FLAGRANT DECEPTION IN THE FORM OF AN IDENTIFICATION OF WHAT IS TO WHAT WOULD BE WELL THAT BE. AND THE TRUTH IS THAT THERE IS ONLY A GLOBAL FLOWS OF MONEY, CAPITAL, INFORMATION; BUT IT DOES NOT FUNCTION AS A RATIONAL AND SOLID GLOBAL FINANCIAL SYSTEM. THAT IS, BY ANY CHANCE, WAS A REALITY, NOT JUST EMPTY TALK, THE CURRENT GLOBAL FINANCIAL AND ECONOMIC CRISIS WOULD UNDOUBTEDLY HAVE BEEN DIFFERENT: IF IT WAS, WOULD BE SOFTER AND MORE READILY.

---

[i] In the centuries-long period (and often still used today), colloquially, as the context requires, synonymic, the definitions: „finance", „money and finance", „public and monetary finance", „financial sector", „financial markets and financial intermediaries (institutions)". Not seldom, in parallel to or instead of them, and uses the term "financial system", in consideration of financial matters at a time when the term is not officially exist. In other words, we often encounter the wording of which impose two conclusions: (1) that before the financial revolution existed finance, financial elements and components, and their structure is not in dispute, and (2) that the mere existence of these elements and component existed formalized financial system, which is not true.

The term "financial system" is a recent. His constitution / codification and recognition forced the modern financial revolution.

Significant changes in the financial performance of existing elements and components, and the advent of many completely new and much more complex, represented a major structural and functional changes in the modern world of finance. To the world in general to work, if not perfect, and that on a relatively satisfactory manner, it is necessary to establish/codify and establish itself as a relatively complete financial system with its own identity. They are not a mere semantic issue that can be ignored, but theirs understanding, at least in general notions, is conditio sine qua non for understanding modern finance, and economic existence and development in contemporary financial environment

[ii] To remind, this general known phrase denote the sudden deregulation of financial markets in the UK, 1986, in time government of Margaret Thatcher. Specifically, it is about changing the rules of the London Stock Exchange, which occurred 27. October 1986. in the sense that were allowed to stockbrokers (and not only stockjobbers) may buy and sell shares for their own account (and not just on behalf of large corporations, monopolists). This led to far-reaching changes: expanding competition by preventing monopolies and cartels that control the securities industry, and an introduction to one of the most important (although seemingly technical) change - the development of electronic, screen-based rather than open-outcry trading.

[iii] From this formulation, who is not any exception, it could be inferred about the undeniable existence of the international financial system. But many facts and many controversial views on the issue, say that the financial system in the international context does not exist, at least not as a system. Moreover, can not speak about the entirely harmonization independent national financial systems neither globally, nor even within the EMU. The fact that there are some international financial institutions such as the BIS, the Financial Stability Forum, the IMF, EBRD and others, as well as a number of codes and rules of conduct, is far from the international entirely financial system. Moreover, these international institutions are not supervisors with command powers on the national level. Their impact is reduced to coordinate and monitoring compliance of certain principles and rules of behavior on national level. If there is a certain power and influence of these institutions, it is conditional, indirect, non-institutional.